dabble lab

MAKE MIND-BLOWING MUSIC VIDEOS

4D An Augmented Reading Experience

by Thomas Kingsley Troupe

Consultant:
Diana L. Rendina, MLIS
Media Specialist, Speaker, Writer
Tampa, FL

CAPSTONE PRESS
a capstone imprint

1 Ask an adult to download the app.

Capstone 4D Education

2 Scan any page with the star.

3 Enjoy your cool stuff!

—— OR ——

Use this password at capstone4D.com

musicvideos.40093

Dabble Lab Books are published by Capstone Press
1710 Roe Crest Drive
North Mankato, Minnesota 56003
www.mycapstone.com

Library of Congress Cataloging-in-Publication Data
Names: Troupe, Thomas Kingsley, author.
Title: Make mind-blowing music videos: 4D an augmented reading experience / by Thomas Kingsley Troupe.
Other titles: 1st ed. Description: North Mankato, Minnesota : Capstone Press, [2020] | Series: Make a movie! 4D | Audience: Age 8-10. | Audience: Grade 4 to 6. Identifiers: LCCN 2019004837|
ISBN 9781543540093 (hardcover) | ISBN 9781543540178 (ebook pdf) Subjects: LCSH: Music videos—Production and direction—Juvenile literature. Classification: LCC PN1992.8.M87 T76 2020 | DDC 780.26/7—dc23 LC record available at https://lccn.loc.gov/2019004837

Editorial Credits
Shelly Lyons, editor; Sarah Bennett, designer; Morgan Walters, media researcher; Katy LaVigne, production specialist

Photo Credits
All photos by Capstone Studio, Karon Dubke, with the exception of: Shutterstock: ArrowStudio, (girls) Cover, 15; Astarina, (movie action) Cover; Can Yesil, (phone) Cover; Darcraft, (rec) Cover; handini_atmodiwiryo, (books) 11; koonsiri boonnak, top right 4; Lightspring, (stage) 45; whatzapa, (music notes) 5; mixform design, 16, 21, 40; Natasha Pankina, design element throughout; ONYXprj, (gadgets) 15, 28-29, 44; paniti Alapon, 38; Ramona Kaulitzki, design element throughout; Rolau Elena, design element throughout; Seth Gallmeyer, (notebook) design element; Shorena Tedliashvili, (film strip) design element; silm, design element throughout; Tono Balaguer, bottom 4; Vissay, (poster) 45; Vyacheslav Sakhatsky, (tripod) 11

All internet sites, apps, and software programs appearing in back matter were available and accurate when this book was sent to press.

Printed and bound in China.
1671

CONTENTS

Music Video Magic

What are music videos?

A guitar wails as the lights go up and a band takes the stage. The drumbeat kicks in. The lead singer grabs the microphone. Is this a rock concert? Nope. It's a music video! Music videos are short movies that are used to promote a song. With flashy visuals and dynamic shots, they're designed to get people excited about a song and the band behind the music.

Music Video Success Guide

Be Patient Filmmaking is something that takes practice. You won't make a perfect music video the first time, the second time, or ever. Practice makes *better*, never perfect.

Plan It Out Even though it seems simple to just show people lip-synching to a song or a band playing instruments, it's a huge help to have a plan in place. Is the video going to tell a story? Will it highlight the band? Will it do a little of both?

Experiment Try new things, including shooting from different angles. Experiment with black and white or color. Make your music video stand out by giving it YOUR flavor and something that will complement the band or singer's music.

What You'll Need

☆ an idea
☆ a song
☆ a storyboard
☆ talent/band
☆ a video camera/ smartphone/tablet
☆ a location
☆ lights
☆ a microphone
☆ a tripod
☆ editing software

Finding Gear

Creating your own music video shouldn't drain your wallet. You can likely find everything you'll need for your production around the house. Don't put your vision on hold until you can buy the best gear. Plenty of great music videos have been made for next to nothing. Use what you have to make music video magic!

Camera Ready

Digital Cameras

One of the most important tools in making your music video is your camera. Find a digital camera that is simple to use and able to record long clips of video. You'll be taking lots of shots of the musicians, so make sure the camera's memory card has plenty of space on it.

Smartphones & Tablets

If you can use a smartphone or a tablet as your camera, you're in luck. Not only are smartphones small and easy to use, many of them have video-editing apps built in. If not, you can always add one. Be sure to have an adult help you download the app you need. Just make sure there's enough memory available for all of your video footage.

Lighting

Besides the camera, you'll need light. Use lamps, overhead lights, whatever you can find to brighten up the scene. Natural light works well too. Keep in mind that sunlight will change throughout the day.

Place your light source out of the camera's range. You don't want to see cords or lights, if possible. Aim the lights at your talent so their faces and instruments are lit up. Try to avoid odd, distracting shadows. You want viewers to focus on the musicians.

Tripods

A tripod is a great tool that helps keep your shots steady. No need to go fancy. You can find inexpensive options out there. Most tripods have adjustable legs and heads that will allow you to change the camera's height.

Want to put your camera somewhere unique? Tabletop tripods let you place cameras on shelves, tables, or pretty much anywhere! If you don't have a tripod, use books or something heavy to keep your camera in place.

phone tripod →

PRO TIP

Don't feel like you HAVE to keep your camera locked onto a tripod. Sometimes going "handheld" will give your video a different feel and will allow you to capture things from many angles.

Find That Song!

Once you have the important gear figured out, find the right song. The song is what you'll build the music video around.

The type of song you pick will likely drive how the video will look and feel. If it's a slow song, you might use long, mellow shots. Fast, rockin', and up-tempo songs mean you'll probably keep things moving and edit lots of different shots. The big rule? There are (mostly) no rules when making a music video!

PRO TIP

If you can, try to use a song that you've created or someone you know has recorded. Songs from popular artists are tricky and can get you in trouble if you don't get permission to use them first!

Idea Factory

Coming up with an idea for a music video is one of the best parts. Do you want to film a band playing music? Want to make a mini-movie that tells a story based on the song's lyrics? Maybe it should be an artsy splash of color and sound?

Keep in mind that you're doing a low/no-budget video. You probably can't have explosions behind the band or really expensive special effects. Think about what you've got to work with and do your best with what you have. Some of the best music videos are really simple and cheap.

PRO TIP

Need some ideas for your music video? Check out some of the videos other people have made. Just make sure to make YOUR video your own!

Script-tastic!

Writing a script for a music video might seem like a waste of time. But even if your video is just going to be a band playing in the middle of an auditorium, it still helps to have some structure to the shoot. If the video is more like a mini-movie, you definitely will want to write out who will say what. You'll also need to write out the action that will take place.

Your script doesn't need to look like a professional Hollywood script. Start with the song's lyrics. Look at the words and decide what you'd like to have happen at each part of the song. If characters will speak in the video, add that to the script too. Scripts can also be broken down into segments of time.

Script for "Too Late"

VERSE ONE—	SCENES—
☑ Wake up! It's time for school.	I wake up. My surprised face! Close-up: Alarm clock;
☐ No PJs, it's time for clothes!	I'm throwing clothes out of my dresser.
☐ Brush my hair and brush my teeth.	Frothy teeth brushing!
☐ Why didn't my alarm ring? It's 9 o'clock, school starts at 8.	Cut away to me shoving books into my backpack.
☐ Oh no! Oh no! I think I'm too late! What will I do today? Oh no!	

PRO TIP

Put check boxes along the side of the song's lyrics. Once you've filmed each part, check off the parts of the song you've captured. You'll know you've got everything when all the boxes are checked.

Storyboard Basics

In addition to a script, it's a great idea to create a storyboard. A storyboard is almost like a comic strip. You'll draw in what each shot for the music video might look like. Think of it like a visual checklist of the things you want to capture.

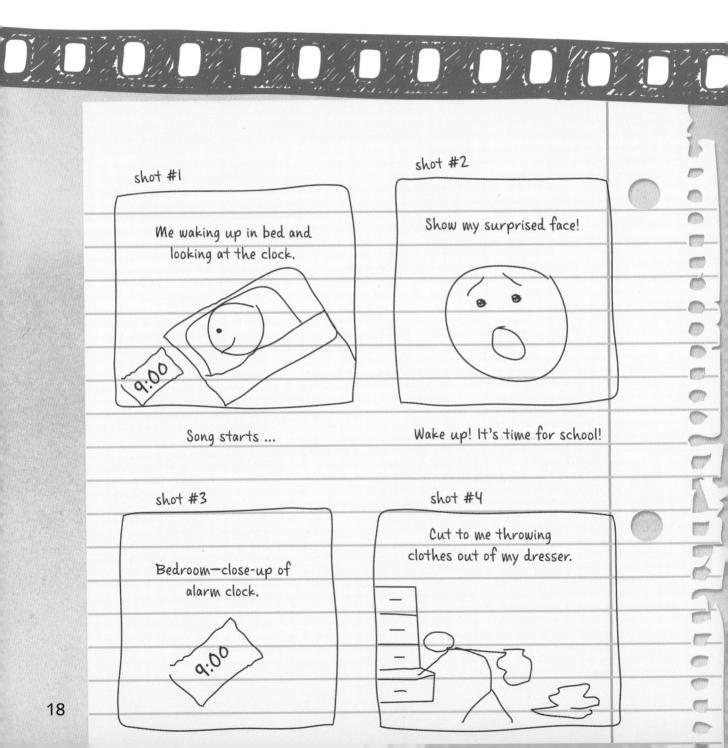

shot #1

Me waking up in bed and looking at the clock.

9:00

Song starts ...

shot #2

Show my surprised face!

Wake up! It's time for school!

shot #3

Bedroom—close-up of alarm clock.

9:00

shot #4

Cut to me throwing clothes out of my dresser.

Don't spend a lot of time making each panel in the storyboard perfect. You can draw stick figures and rough sketches to fill in the panels. The important thing is to make sure to draw all the shots that will make up your music video.

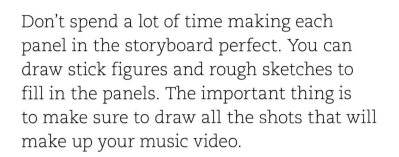

PRO

Find some space each drawing to write in a little bit of the lyrics from the song. This way, you'll be able to keep track of how long each shot will take. It'll also make editing your video much easier!

shot #5

Cut to bathroom:
Me brushing my teeth.

Brush my hair
and brush my teeth.

shot #6

Shot of me shoving books
into my backpack.

Why didn't my alarm ring? It's
9 o'clock, school starts at 8.

shot #7

I'm freaking out!

shot #8

CHORUS STARTS:
We're all lip-synching
in the garage.

19

Band Together

Most music videos feature the artists and musicians who've created the song. They're basically the stars of the show and should be in the video, if possible.

If the musicians can't be in the video, ask your friends to do some acting. They could stand in and pretend to play instruments. If the music video is more story-based than onstage performance, they could play characters. Your only limit is your imagination!

Filming with friends can be lots of fun! ☺ ☺ ☺

PRO TIP

Don't have anyone to appear in the video? Film random shots of things happening in your house or neighborhood. Chances are, when you add the music to it, it'll feel like a music video.

Location, Location!

You've got all of your gear together, your script and storyboard are in great shape, and you have people willing to help make the video. Now what? Time to find a location!

Try and find a unique, interesting place for your viewers to look at. Maybe there's a big garage with a bunch of old things in it, or a basement with really funky wallpaper. Avoid using a place that's plain and forgettable. You want people to remember your music video! If the location isn't in your neighborhood, ask an adult to drive you there. The best part? You won't have to carry all of your equipment across town!

PRO TIP

Take time to find the perfect location. You'll need a place with power outlets and enough room for equipment and props. You'll want the place to be visually interesting too. The location will drive the look of the video, so it's worth the time to find a great spot!

Get Permission

You've found the perfect location for your shoot. All you need to do is set up and get the camera rolling, right? Wrong! Nothing can shut down a video shoot faster than being told you're not allowed to film somewhere.

Make sure you're allowed to film in the area you want to shoot. Ask permission, even if it's a friend's house, your grandma's attic, or the local park. Some people are very picky about what happens on their property. There are also locations that will charge a fee for filming there.

And ... Action!

At long last, it's time to shoot your video! Consult your script and storyboard to determine which shot you'd like to film first. Turn on your lights, set your camera on the tripod, and ask your talent to move to their places for the first shot.

Let the band or actors know what they need to do for each shot. If they're going to mimic playing music, consider playing that part of the song. Film the same part a few times until you feel like you've got the shots you want.

Let's try again. This time look at the camera.

Awesome! ☺

☑ Wake up!
  It's time for school.

☐ No PJs,
  it's time for clothes!

☐ Brush my hair and
  brush my teeth.

☑ Why didn't my alarm
  ring? It's 9 o'clock,
  school starts at 8.

☑ Oh no! Oh no!
  I think I'm too late!
  What will I do today?
  Oh no!

PRO TIP

There's no rule that says you need to film the scenes in order. As long as you keep track of what you're shooting and what you need, shoot in any order you want!

Shot Options

To keep your video interesting, you need some variety! Adjust the camera, shoot different things in the room, or shoot from different angles. Try some of these camera shots:

Pan and Tilt Shots—moving the camera from left to right (pan) or moving the camera up or down (tilt)

pan shot (left to right)

tilt shot (up or down)

PRO TIP

Capture as much as possible when shooting. Don't worry about having too much footage. You can decide what to keep and what to cut later. Having more than you need is better than needing more than you have!

Exterior Shot—filming the location where the video is taking place; if you're filming inside a garage, for example, film a bit of the outside of the building; exterior shots help your audience get a clear sense of the location

Close-Up—getting up close and personal to the object, place, or person you're filming

Zoom—using the built-in zoom feature to move closer to (zoom in) or farther away from (zoom out) the person, place, or object you're filming; this is sometimes a sliding bar or a button on a digital camera

wide-angle
(pull camera back)

Wide-Angle—pulling the camera back so more of the scene is shown

Me waking up and looking at the clock ⇨ shot from the side of the bed

Coverage

While shooting the video, you'll want to keep a few things in mind. First, make sure you've got all the shots that were planned in your script and storyboard. Second, make sure you've got enough coverage.

One way to make sure you've got coverage is to shoot the same shot but from another angle. Maybe you do a close-up of a character getting out of bed. Once you have that shot, pull the camera back or change the angle. Shoot it again from a new position. Now you've got coverage and plenty of options when editing.

Same scene ⇨ shot from above

PRO TIP

Be sure to give your talent and friends breaks from time to time. A video can take a while, so it's good to have snacks and water available. Treat your crew right, and they'll stick around to help!

Cutaways

Giving the audience a break from seeing the same thing for three to four minutes is important. Humans tend to have short attention spans, so between shots of the band, it's sometimes nice to cut away to shots of other things or people.

Your location should give you plenty of ideas. Maybe film a close-up of a guitar or ukulele. Record something happening outside or even an interesting object in the room. Again, it's all about having options when you edit.

Cutting Room

Do you like putting together puzzles? If so, you're going to love editing. After all the filming is done and you're satisfied with the shots you captured, it's time to put the pieces into place. Now is the time to make your music video come to life!

The first step in the editing process is to upload the video you've shot to your editing app/software. Since this is a music video, you'll also want to upload the song. The song is going to be your guide while you're editing.

PRO TIP

Look through your shots and try to number them in the order they should appear. This will help when you arrange the pieces in your music video puzzle.

Rough Cut

Play the song while in the editing program to get started. This will help you visualize the music video. If you need the wide shot of the band for your opening first few seconds, find that footage. Drop the best version of each shot where it belongs during the song, then move to the next piece. Your storyboard and script should help you locate which shot goes where.

When you've got all the shots into place, you have a "rough cut" of your music video. Congrats! Now watch the whole thing. Keep in mind that it's going to be clunky. Take notes about areas you want to trim and change.

PRO TIP

The rough cut is just that—ROUGH. Don't be discouraged if it doesn't line up perfectly with the lyrics or music. Watching the rough cut is just the step that gets everything into position.

Fine-Tuning

Now that you've seen the rough version of your video, it's time to fine-tune it. Cut out the parts that don't work. Edit in some of your alternate takes, and keep each shot short and sweet. Remember, viewers will get bored seeing the same thing for too long.

If you can, time your edits with the beats in a song. If there's a big drum hit, jump to another shot. If you can edit your video in time with the music, it'll seem like you planned it that way all along!

PRO TIP

Never permanently delete any of your footage! Even if you cut something from the final video, it's good to keep it in case you need it later.

Sound and Visual Effects

The bulk of the sound for your music video will be the song you've chosen. However, there might be places where a character speaks or a sound effect is needed. If so, you can record dialogue or drop a sound clip into the video. Just remember, the song is the star. Be careful not to overdo the effects.

A lot of editing programs allow you to change the color of the video. Want to make it look old-fashioned? Try changing it to black and white. Some filters can give the video a scratchy, true film look. Experiment! And remember, you can always change it back if you don't like it. If your video is more like a story, consider fading between scenes. It will give the music video a more movie-like feel, instead of clunky, rapid cuts.

⇧
SOUND EFFECT
Record running water, and then add the sound effect to the toothbrushing clip.

Add Credits

Unlike movies and documentaries, music videos don't really have credits that scroll at the end. Instead, they tend to put artist information in the lower left corner at the beginning of the video.

> **Example:**
> ARTIST: Noah Gassman
> SONG: "Too Late"
> DIRECTOR: Jaden J.
> CREW: Lydia and Maya

Having credits at the front end of the video lets viewers know the name of the group and the title of the song. They might love the music and video enough that they'll want to buy the song for themselves!

PRO TIP

Don't forget to thank the people who helped you create the video. Add credits for each of your crew members too.

Artist: Noah Gassman
Song: "Too Late"
Director: Jaden J.
Crew: Lydia and Maya

0:17 / 0:24

Settings

Center Stage

Sharing Your Video

Now it's time to share your video with your soon-to-be fans. Make a big deal about it! Have a premiere night at your house and invite your family to watch it. If your friends have made some videos too, turn the night into a video showcase. Want people around the world to watch it? Get permission from all the people in the video first. Then see if your parents/guardians are OK with you uploading it to the internet (YouTube, Vimeo).

That's a Wrap!

Now that you've created your first music video, go make another. Using what you've learned, you can make something even better than your original. With a new song in your head, you can try some new tricks to bring the music to life. Just keep practicing. In no time, you'll have bands begging you to make their next music video!

PRO TIP

If you don't want to use your real name (or other identifying information), be sure to remove it from the video before posting it online. Remember not to upload videos with music you don't have permission to use!

Meet Your Film Instructor

 **Thomas Kingsley Troupe** is an amateur filmmaker who has been making goofy movies and videos since he was in high school. Thomas has worked in the visual effects department for a handful of Hollywood movies and shows. He has also written and directed a number of short films for the 48 Hour Film Fest & Z Fest contests and loves creating funny videos with his own sons at home. Thomas says, "Making movies is the BEST. It can be a lot of work, but finishing a movie to show to your friends and family is WORTH IT!"

Read More

Farrell, Dan, and Donna Bamford. *The Movie Making Book: Skills & Projects to Learn & Share.* Chicago: Chicago Review Press, 2017.

Grabham, Tim. *Video Ideas.* New York: DK Publishing, 2018.

Internet Sites

Chrome Music Lab
https://musiclab.chromeexperiments.com/Experiments

National Geographic Kids Photo Tips and Tricks
https://kids.nationalgeographic.com/explore/tips-tricks/

Glossary

app—a computer application

complement—to complete or enhance something

coverage—the amount of footage and different camera angles used to capture a scene

dynamic—constantly changing

edit—to cut and rearrange pieces of film to make a movie or TV program

premiere—the first public performance of a film, play, or work of music or dance

rough cut—the first version of a movie after early editing

scene—a part of a story, play, or movie that shows what is happening in one place and time

script—the story for a play, movie, or TV show

segment—a separate piece of something

storyboard—a series of drawings that shows the plot of a TV show or movie

tempo—the speed or rhythm of a piece of music

Apps and Software

Green Screen, by Do Ink—helps users create videos using the green screen effect

iMovie, by Apple—an app to create your own movies

Movie Maker 10, by Microsoft—a full movie-making software for all budding artists

Index